How to Deal with OBESITY

Lynette Robbins

PowerKiDS press™

New York

Published in 2010 by The Rosen Publishing Group, Inc.
29 East 21st Street, New York, NY 10010

First Edition

Editor: Joanne Randolph
Book Design: Kate Laczynski
Photo Researcher: Jessica Gerweck

Photo Credits: Cover, pp. 1, 8 (background and pyramid), 16 Shutterstock.com; p. 4 © Jason Horowitz/zefa/Corbis; p. 6 © Achim Pohl/Peter Arnold, Inc.; p. 10 © Ronnie Kaufman/zefa/Corbis; p. 12 Stock4B/Getty Images; p. 14 © Karen Kasmauski/Corbis; p. 18 © Alan Levenson/Age Fotostock; p. 20 Peter Dazeley/Getty Images.

Library of Congress Cataloging-in-Publication Data

Robbins, Lynette.
  How to deal with obesity / Lynette Robbins. — 1st ed.
     p. cm. — (Kids' health)
  Includes index.
  ISBN 978-1-4042-8143-1 (lib. bdg.) — ISBN 978-1-4358-3423-1 (pbk.) — ISBN 978-1-4358-3424-8 (6-pack)
  1. Obesity in children—Juvenile literature. I. Title.
  RJ399.C6R63 2010
  618.92'398—dc22
                                        2009008902

Manufactured in the United States of America

CONTENTS

4

Sarah's Problem

Sarah was a chubby baby. When she was a toddler, everyone said her extra weight was just "baby fat." In kindergarten, Sarah was so overweight that she had trouble keeping up with the other kids when they had races or played tag. By second grade, her weight problem was even more **serious**. The other kids in Sarah's class called her names because of her weight.

Sarah has a medical condition called obesity. Sarah weighs much more than she should for her height. People who are obese are not healthy. They often do not feel good about their bodies. The good news is that a person who is obese does not have to stay that way!

Some people are overweight, which means they are heavier than they should be for their height and age. When people become seriously overweight, they are obese.

6

What Is Obesity?

Food is fuel for your body, just as gasoline is fuel for a car. Food gives you energy to do things. Most people use up the energy they get from food. Then they eat more food to get more energy.

Some people eat more food than their bodies can use. When a person eats more food than his body needs, the extra food is stored as fat. A person who has a little bit too much extra fat on his body is overweight. When a person has a great deal of extra fat, then he is obese. A person who is obese may have problems doing everyday things, such as walking up stairs, running, or even sleeping.

This girl chose to eat ice cream to give her energy while she did her homework. Eating high-fat, sugary foods, such as ice cream, can cause a person to gain weight, though.

You Are What You Eat

Have you ever kept eating, even though your stomach was full? People who are obese often eat too much food. They may put too much food on their plates. They may take a second helping of food or even a third. They may snack a lot between meals.

Eating too much of the wrong kinds of foods also causes obesity. Such foods include candy, doughnuts, potato chips, and soda. These foods have a lot of sugar, fat, and **carbohydrates**. None of these things are good for your body in large amounts. Eating a lot of pasta, bread, and other foods that are high in carbohydrates can also cause a person to gain weight.

This chart shows the kinds of foods people should be eating each day. A healthy person needs a balance of carbohydrates, fruits and vegetables, and meat and dairy products.

Not Enough Exercise

Jason is obese. When Jason gets home from school, he goes right to the TV. He sits down and watches his favorite shows. Then he plays video games until dinner.

It does not take much energy to sit in front of the TV. Like Jason, many children are obese because they spend too much time in front of the TV or doing other **sedentary** activities. Being active takes more energy. When you ride your bike, play sports, or take walks, you are using up more energy than when you watch TV. People who do not get enough **exercise** are in danger of becoming obese. If you get off the couch and start moving, not only will you lose weight, but you will feel better, too.

One of the best ways to stop obesity from taking over your life is to be active. This boy started taking karate class a few weeks ago, and he already feels healthier!

All in the Family

Poor eating habits and not getting enough exercise are the most common causes of obesity. However, some people are obese for other reasons. If you are gaining weight even with a healthy diet and exercise, you may want to check with your doctor. Some people have a **disorder** or illness that makes them gain weight easily. Other people may become obese because they are taking medicine that causes them to gain weight.

Obesity also runs in families. That means that a person is more likely to be obese if her parents are obese. However, not all people with obese parents are obese themselves.

If obesity runs in your family, get healthy together! Joseph and his mother do exercises on the beach a few mornings a week.

14

The Dangers of Childhood Obesity

Anna is obese. Because of her obesity, she now has **asthma**. Anna's asthma makes it hard for her to breathe. Anna's doctor is worried that her obesity may also lead to **diabetes**. Diabetes is a serious illness. If Anna gets diabetes, she may have to give herself shots to keep from getting too much sugar in her blood.

Like Anna, people who are obese are at risk for getting other serious illnesses, such as asthma, diabetes, and liver problems. They may also develop **sleep apnea**. Sleep apnea makes it hard to sleep well. Obese people may also have conditions that can lead to **strokes** and heart attacks.

If you are obese, it is not too late to change your life! Pay attention to food labels at the store, and choose foods that are low in sugar and fat.

Obesity at School

Kevin does not like going to school. Other kids tease him. They call him mean names because he is obese. At recess, Kevin does not play with the other children. He has trouble breathing when he runs. Being obese makes it hard for him to play sports. How do you think Kevin feels?

Obese children cannot run and play as other children can. They are often teased by their classmates for being overweight. They may be bullied and picked on. An obese child may have trouble making friends. Being treated badly by other kids can hurt a child's feelings and hurt his self-esteem, or the way he feels about himself.

If other kids make fun of you because of your weight, you know it does not feel good. Do not change for those people, though. Become healthier for yourself!

Get Active!

If you are obese, you do not have to stay that way! There are many things you can do to lose weight and improve your health. One of the best things you can do is to get your body moving. Try to do something active every day.

Instead of watching TV, try taking a walk. Walking is a great way to start exercising. There are many other things you can do, too. You can shoot baskets, go swimming, take **martial arts** classes, or ride your bike. You could even turn on the radio and dance around your house or bedroom. Any activity that gets you moving will work. What kinds of things do you like to do?

Finding something you enjoy doing will make it easier to be active. It will also make it easier to stick with the activity.

Make Wise Choices

Eating the right amount of healthy food is important. When you eat smaller amounts, or portions, of healthy food, you will feel better.

The trick to eating smaller portions is to listen to your body and stop eating when you are no longer hungry. If you eat more slowly, it will give your body time to know it is full. It can help to stop eating halfway through a meal and ask yourself if you are still hungry. If the answer is no, stop eating. It is also important to choose healthy foods, such as fruits and vegetables. If you are obese, your parents might take you to a doctor or a **nutritionist**.

A nutritionist can teach you about healthy foods and help you make good choices. A green salad is a good choice because it has lots of vitamins and very little fat or sugar.

Do Not Live with Obesity!

It is no fun to be obese, and it is bad for your health, too. If you are obese, you may need to ask for help. Your parents can help by keeping healthy food in the house. With fewer unhealthy foods around, you will make better choices about what to eat. Your parents can also help find fun ways for you to stay active. They might also take you to a doctor, **therapist**, or nutritionist for more ideas about how you can live a healthier life.

When you start exercising and eating healthier foods, you will feel better. You will have more energy. You will be able to do more. You will feel better about yourself, too. Are you ready to be healthy?

GLOSSARY

asthma (AZ-muh) A condition that makes it hard for a person to breathe.

carbohydrates (kar-boh-HY-drayts) The main element in foods made mostly from plants, such as potatoes and bread.

diabetes (dy-uh-BEE-teez) A sickness in which a person's body cannot take in sugar and starch normally.

disorder (dis-OR-der) A sickness or medical condition.

exercise (EK-ser-syz) Moving your body in ways that help you get or stay fit.

martial arts (MAR-shul ARTS) Kinds of self-defense or fighting that are practiced as sports.

nutritionist (noo-TRIH-shuh-nist) A person who teaches others about healthy eating.

sedentary (SEH-den-ter-ee) Staying in the same place.

serious (SIR-ee-us) Important or bad.

sleep apnea (SLEEP AP-nee-uh) A condition in which a person stops breathing for a short period of time while sleeping.

strokes (STROHKS) What happens to people when blood vessels, or the parts that carry blood in your body, break or when the vessels get blocked in the brain.

therapist (THER-uh-pist) A person who is trained to work with people to help them understand their feelings.

INDEX

WEB SITES

Due to the changing nature of Internet links, PowerKids Press has developed an online list of Web sites related to the subject of this book. This site is updated regularly. Please use this link to access the list: www.powerkidslinks.com/heal/obesity/